REAL ESTATE

INVESTING

IN THE HOOD

EVERYTHING YOU NEED TO KNOW TO CLOSE THE DEAL!

By:

Mickey Frazier Sr

TABLE OF CONTENTS

IS THE BUSINESS OF REAL ESTATE FOR YOU?

For many years now, plenty of people that are wealthy have gotten that way through investing in real estate. Real estate investments are one of the things that can bring ongoing financial profits every month. When it increases in value, your investment becomes that much more important and profitable.

You can get your money's worth when the value of your real estate investment increases. However, people that are interested in real estate investment need to know that it is more than just making money.

There are many things you need to consider if you are interested in investing in real estate, in particular residential real estate. There is no doubt that you can be very wealthy with this. However, you will have to stay in it for the long haul in order to make it work for you.

If this is your first foray with this, you will want to weigh your options as far as how you will purchase your initial property. Not a lot of people have the entire amount up front to purchase the property with cash.

So, instead of saving, some people will go ahead and get a loan in order to get started. Some experts say that it is better to wait and save your money first. This way, the monthly income that comes in will go to you instead of the lender. You will also be able to build wealth quicker by paying the entire amount in cash.

However, it is still possible that a bank will loan you the money you need in order to get the property. If you go this route, make sure that you have some backup funds in the event you get in a financial rut. At least you will still be able to pay on the loan.

Of course, the better situation is to have all of the money up front and pay cash outright for it. After that, you would only be responsible for repairs, maintenance, taxes and other miscellaneous items.

When considering a property for investment purposes, you will need to know how much it will cost you in taxes.

Every year, you will have to do this or you could find yourself with a lien on your home. In addition to that, you will need to determine a monthly rent amount for whoever you allow to stay there.

Some investors will go through a rental or management company to get their rent. This can release some of the duties from your schedule. On the other hand, you will have to shell out more money to the company for outsourcing.

Only when you are financially able, should you do this. As a beginner investor, you should be responsible for collecting the rent and other fees as deemed appropriate.

Make sure that you have enough money put away for repairs, expected and unexpected. You never know when something will stop working in a split second. It's better to be prepared that unprepared for things such as this.

WHY PEOPLE INVEST IN REAL ESTATE AND WHY THEY WIN

Many people know that real estate investing is very lucrative. For that reason alone, will make people want to get their share of the pie. They know that this is a great way to build wealth, not only for them, but they can also pass it down to their future generations.

In addition to having monthly rental income, there are other factors that contribute as to why people invest in real estate. Some of them include:

- With appreciation of rental properties, there will be increased value. In turn, this could help with the selling and reinvesting in properties that already have a higher value. Appreciation of rental properties can also make way for an equity line of credit for future use.

- Speaking of equity, you as an investor can invest in sweat equity, which involves making improvements to your real estate property. It doesn't have to be so far out where you end up spending a lot of money.

  This can help the value of your property go up faster than it would have if you had not made improvements. So, if you spend $3,000 on cosmetics and miscellaneous items, then the value of the property could be double or more of the amount you spent on improvements.

- Being a real estate investor during inflation times is not necessarily a bad thing. Even though rental payments increase during this time, your mortgage loan payments should remain the same. Because of this, you can have an increase in cash flow.

  Another thing about inflation is that you can also gain more renters (if you have vacancies) because some people may not be able to secure mortgages during that time. Since you will have a greater demand for renters, the rent will also increase. This is part of the agenda of supply and demand.

- Using "Other People's Money", or "OPM", is a good reason for people to invest in real estate. You can find a bank that will secure a loan for you for your real estate investment(s). The better your credit, the better chance you have of securing a good fixed rate loan with low interest rates.

  You can also look at zero-down loans, but that can be more risky. You would have to pay more in your mortgage payments because you didn't include a down payment. So when the property appreciates, it will benefit you along with the monthly cash flow.

- Real estate investing is considered a business. You can use the expenses from it and deduct them from your taxes. Anything that you purchased, had repaired, any fees and anything else related to the investment in question.

  Even if you have properties that are out of the regional area where you have to travel, those expenses can also be deducted from your taxes. If nothing else, being able to deduct expenses from your taxes is like a marriage made in heaven.

- Have you heard of getting cash that is tax free? Say you have an increase in rentals and you end up having a positive cash flow. The surplus can be used for other things. If it's the right time, you may think about wanting to refinance the rental properties.

  If you do that, you could secure a higher mortgage about $20 - $50,000 more than the original. You would pay off the initial mortgage, and have a nice surplus afterwards. The surplus would be considered tax-free money.

- The 1031 Exchange is named after Section1031 in the Internal Revenue Code. It discusses how real estate investors can hold off on capital gains taxes when selling one of their properties. There are three conditions that have to be met before the 1031 Exchange can go into effect:

1. It is a real estate property investment and not a main residence for the investor.

2. The real estate property can be swapped for a property of the same or similar kind.

3. In regard to replacement, there must be certain time frames in place and adhered to.

When an investor uses profits from another property sale and invest them in another property, they can hold off on capital gains for future real estate transactions. More than likely, the investor will work on getting additional equity and more income and profits from additional property rentals.

03

DOING REAL ESTATE INVESTMENTS AS PASSIVE OR RESIDUAL INCOME

The money from real estate investing can be used as passive or residual income. Either way, you will consistently have money coming in from your property rental(s). There are some things that you need to know in order to keep the money coming in.

In order to start the wealth process with real estate investing, get one property first. Seek one that does not require a lot of work and is suitable for renting out to prospective tenants. You can look for foreclosures in addition to other types of homes.

People can get foreclosed homes for a steal, usually at auctions. The banks are desperately trying to get rid of these homes because it will be a loss for them if they keep them. You will still be able to make an investment once you get it fixed up and suitable for living purposes.

If you stick with the real estate investments, you will eventually profit from them. Don't look for an overnight windfall. You have to build your wealth with real estate investing. There will be those times when the economy and real estate market will change. However, you will still be able to profit from it, as long as you hang in there.

When you are making passive or residual income, you are making money when you own rental properties and not having to do the work on the property itself. Rental properties can help to keep money in your pocket.

Eventually, you will make enough money from these properties so that you will not have to work a full-time job anymore. For the most part, that is a goal for most people. They key to building wealth is to stay with it and not get discouraged if you have patterns of lack of rental income. There will be some properties that will generate income all the time, while others may be spotty.

Your goal is to make you and the bank happy by bringing in constant income and not having to work long hours for little pay. If you like that idea than Real Estate Investment Trusts (REITS) may be a real estate passive investment to investigate.

04

WHY REAL ESTATE INVESTING CONTINUES TO HAVE A MARKET

There will always be businesses that will thrive in their season. There are others that will thrive for a moment, and then they fail and end up closing shop. For those who are interested in real estate investing, the same thought may cross their minds. Of course, you have to make sure that you are in the right place at the right time to get properties and get tenants in them.

Like everything else, there is a rise and fall in the real estate market in general. Even with that, you can still benefit from real estate investing. In fact, when the economy is not at its greatest, this becomes some of the best times for potential real estate investors to get great deals for investment properties.

The prices of properties are lower, because the banks want to sell and get rid of them. This can be a great deal for those who can get in the market quickly to snatch up those homes and use them as rental properties. There will always be someone that is looking for a place to live.

Another thing about the market is that you still have some stability, even with a downturn in the economy, as described above. Don't think that when there are economic downturns, that it is the end of the world. It isn't. People don't realize that it is one of the best times for people to purchase property at an affordable price and sometimes a real steal.

Back in the days of the wild, Wild West, when easterners traveled across this vast country looking for opportunity in the newly opened territories, they were often referred to as a 'tenderfoot'.

This wasn't a complimentary term but it was a rather apt one. The easterners wore 'city' shoes that weren't designed to withstand the rigors of the western terrain. Their hats didn't have wide brims to protect them from the sun and their clothing wasn't made of tough material like denim.

These new westerners didn't know how to take care of themselves and because they didn't know where and what the dangers were they didn't have any idea how to avoid them. If you are just beginning to consider the idea of investing in real estate you are a tenderfoot and you do need some instruction to avoid losing your shirt...and probably your pants, hat and boots, as well.

First you will need to determine what your strategy will be in real estate investing. Do you want to buy a property, fix it up and sell it quickly or do you want to buy a property, hold it and wait for the market to increase? Do you want to deal with renters? All of these questions are ones that you need to answer before you invest in any piece of real estate.

You will need to learn how to investigate the value of properties yourself. It isn't fair to use the time of a real estate agent and have them show you property after property while you try to look for a good real estate investment.

There are several online sites that are helpful in determining the real value of real estate. DO NOT rely on tax values. They are not reliable and they are not accurate either. Zillow.com and Realtor.com and other sites have great information but do not use them as official sources.

After you have learned how to determine property values yourself and have chosen a real estate agent that you can work with, the next thing that you need is a good broker that you can also work with. Ask your real estate agent for the names of three mortgage brokers.

Then you will need to find out what interest rates and closing costs each one charges. (Check out your local bank or credit union as well). Take copies of your three credit reports and choose a sample property for each broker to run hard numbers on.

Now you are ready to actually make your first investment. You want to choose the lowest price house in the best possible neighborhood to put a contract on.

Let's say the cheapest two-bedroom house in the best neighborhood in Las Vegas costs $100,000 and the next cheapest, comparable home is listed for $140,000. If you buy the home that is priced at $100,000, you can raise your price to $130,000 the next day and make a dandy little profit if you flip it.

Now let's talk about closing the deal. First show the seller your pre-qualification letter from your lender. Then get the required inspections for termites and get your appraisal. Once you have all of your 'ducks in a row' so to speak, it takes about 30 days to make the final close.

A note here about any renovations or repairs that you might want to make to the property: Before you close, you might want to think about a Purchase and Renovate loan. A Purchase and Renovate loan wraps the cost of construction up in the loan so you don't have many out-of-pocket expenses. This may require an estimate from a general contractor and plans from an architect as well.

Okay, now let's go back to the first thing that you needed to do and that was to determine your strategy. Now is the time for you to execute that strategy that you have used to invest in this real estate. If you bought it with the strategy of flipping it when the market went up then you just simply wait.

If you bought it with the strategy of renovating and then selling then it is time to start your renovations. On the other hand, if you bought it with the strategy of renting it, it is time to start looking for tenants.

You see, the point of having a strategy for profiting from the purchase of any piece of real estate must be your first decision because everything that comes after that is dependent upon it.

05

PROFITING WITH REAL ESTATE INVESTMENTS IN THE HOOD WITH BETTER LOCATIONS, GOOD LOCATIONS AND GREAT LOCATIONS

One of the most, if not the most important thing to know about real estate investments is to make sure that you will have a consistent cash flow. If you don't have a consistent cash flow coming in, then you'll have a difficult time creating wealth in real estate investing.

In addition to having cash flow, there are some ways that you can profit from real estate investments. Let me explain some of them:

- Having rental properties and getting income from them is one of the best known ways to profit and keep a consistent cash flow going. The more rental properties you have, the better chance you have of creating sufficient wealth streams for you and your family. The good thing about this is that even though there are risks, with a market downturn, money will still flow in.

- Have you thought about paying off your mortgage? Well, now may be a good time to start. The more you pay off, the more your equity increases. If need be, the equity can be used for other things.

- If you can afford to get an equity loan, the money could be used for investing in other properties. Keep in mind that you don't want to get in over your head with more debt, so only do this if you can make the loan payments without any problems.

- If you want to get a better price for your property, you may want to spruce it up a bit. Make some upgrades to it so that it will look presentable. This is a great way to increase value and prospective renters will also see the value in what you have accomplished.

- Most investors are not interested in investing in urban real estate. This means that there is a wide open opportunity for those who ARE interested in investing in urban real estate. You will likely hear umpteen reasons why you should NOT invest in urban real estate so let me give you a few good reasons why you SHOULD invest in urban real estate.

- First let's discuss the pricing of urban real estate. If you keep your 'ear to the ground' so to speak you can find some real hidden gems in the urban real estate market. Not every low price is a good deal, of course, and just like with every real estate investment that you ever make, you should be certain that you do your homework.

- Really great deals turn up in every real estate market for one reason or another. Don't miss those terrific investment opportunities simply because the property is in an urban area. Single family houses and condos make great urban rentals.

- Then there are the Section 8 tenants to be considered. Here is an obvious advantage to investing in urban properties. Government subsidized housing is a 21st century reality and under Section 8 the government pays a full 80% of the monthly rent. These renters are often referred to as 'Section 8 tenants'. There is, of course, always a waiting list of potential renters and they all want to move into YOUR urban investment property. If used properly, the Section 8 program can be a landlord's best friend. It takes a lot of the risk out of collecting rent.

- That adds up to a very nice and sure monthly income for you. Renters don't always pay their rent but the government does send checks on time and in full thus eliminating much of the rent collection hassle.

Let's not overlook the fix and flip opportunity afforded by urban real estate investments. Okay, let's face it. Today's real estate market could be better a lot better but just because the over-all market doesn't seem to be all that healthy and do for a correction at the moment that doesn't mean that there aren't some great fix and flip opportunities out there and particularly in the urban areas.

The trick to making a profit on an urban property is to sell with incentives included and, if it is a rental property, with a tenant already in residence.

Don't forget about the good old government of the United States of America. The government funds projects to rehab entire neighborhoods in urban areas and they do soon a regular basis. The local government gets funding and usually offers attractive incentives to developers and home owners investing in these urban neighborhoods.

Not only that but you can some really astounding interest rate offers that will let you keep your money in your pocket and out of and danger at all. This creates a win/win/win situation. The government gets to spend money which they seem to do so well. The inhabitants of the neighborhood get better housing and you make a nice profit. Everybody wins!

There is the tired old real estate saying, "The only three things that matter in real estate are location, location and location." That really is NOT necessarily true. Do you remember playing the board game Monopoly when you were a kid? Remember those first little properties that were located right at the beginning of the game?

They were cheap. They were REALLY cheap. If you bought one of those just out of the gate, so to speak, you could have a hotel up on it almost immediately and every player in the game was going to have to land on it and pay you. It was a pretty good location but not an expensive one. It was one that you could afford to make improvements on quickly.

Remember? Think of investing in urban real estate like you would think of investing in Baltic Avenue or Mediterranean Avenue. You don't pay much for the property but improvements don't cost much either and you can make a profit easily and quickly. It was good strategy for Monopoly and it is a good strategy for real live urban real estate investing.

Urban property investments meet all of the criteria for sound real estate investing.

There is a good rental market in an urban area. There are lots of people who need housing and that housing is very often government subsidized. Urban property is usually low priced and can even be purchased at extremely attractive interest rates as well.

The market is stable in urban neighborhoods. There isn't a boom or bust mentality. Demand is not likely to decrease anytime soon. As long as inventory is high, urban property will thrive.

Investing in urban property can be a very good decision but you should always do your homework before you invest. According to the old real estate saying, "The only three things that matter in real estate are location, location and location." The fact is that a ten bedroom, eight bath home with cathedral ceilings and a swimming pool that is sitting next to a garbage dump is nearly worthless.

On the other hand a little one bedroom, one bath shack sitting in the middle of downtown Dallas would be worth a small fortune. So you can see that the location is of the utmost importance when you are considering a piece of real estate to invest in.

What is it that makes the location of a piece of real estate valuable? The answer is fairly simply really. The value is based on nothing more than the desirability factor. Desirability is a fluctuating intangible that is really hard to nail down.

Property that is totally undesirable to one person might be just the next person's dream- come-true. And this phenomenon is true for real estate investors and for home buyers and for renters. It is true for all aspects of the real estate market.

The main point for any real estate investor to consider first is what their strategy will be for making a profit on a property. Buying is only half of the equation and whether the location of the property is good or bad depends upon that profit strategy.

For example: If an investor is going to invest in a property with the intention of just waiting for the market to go up, prime real estate is probably the very best choice. Locations that are near entertainment centers or developing areas would be best because the likely hood that the property will increase in value simply by waiting is a pretty good bet.

On the other hand, if an investor is going to invest in a property with the intention of renting it and making a monthly income from it, he might be better off to look into urban properties. Urban properties wouldn't be considered 'prime' real estate but they are 'prime' rental properties.

Then there are real estate investors who are handy with their hands. They can make repairs and renovations to rundown properties themselves, sell it for a great deal more than their purchase price and make a very nice profit. The location that these kinds of real estate investors often find the best is in neighborhoods that are made up of mid priced homes in working neighborhoods.

There are many factors that real estate investors consider when they are deciding which property to invest in. One factor can be what I call the 'snob' factor.

It's strange but people will pay a lot more money for a small property in the 'right' neighborhood than they will for a larger property in a less desirable neighborhood. However one person's definition of a 'good' neighborhood will not be anywhere close to another person's definition of a 'good neighborhood.

Then there is the 'visibility' factor. If a neighborhood or an area has become famous or even infamous, property values rise regardless of the location. Convenience is another factor when considering the desirability of the location of a piece of property. People do like to live close to where they work and where their children attend school.

Rising gas prices just might work wonders for real estate prices in inner cities.

The desirability of the location of any piece of real estate can be determined by a great many different factors for real estate investors and for home buyers and renters. If the location is desirable for the investor's purposes he will invest.

If the location is desirable for a home buyer's purposes then he will buy. If the location is desirable for a renter's purposes then he will rent. So basically, you can roll all of the various factors for determining whether a location is good or bad into one simple work; desirability. We are a nation of individuals. We all see things from a different point of view. Look around. There are people living everywhere. They live in big cities, small towns and in urban and rural areas. Who can determine what a 'good' location really is?

There is a proverb that says, "Beauty is in the eye of the beholder". The modern version would be 'whatever floats your boat is good'. In real estate it would translate to 'if the location serves your purpose then it's a good location'.

06

PURCHASING REAL ESTATE THAT IS UNDERVALUED IN HOT MARKETS

At first, starting out in real estate investing, you may think that you need to get a higher priced piece of property. However, that is not the case. In fact, most investors prefer to use the method of buy low and sell high.

That is the way they can profit from purchasing property that is considered to be undervalued. Not only does it save you money, it also can also pay off for you in the end.

There are different reasons why a potential property might sell below its actual value:

- Foreclosed property

- Investor wants to get rid of it

- Property passed down from previous generation(s)

- Property is in bad shape and need lots of repairs

- Personal events in family where they can no longer take care of the property

- Excessive damage from inclement weather or fire

The reasons above are the ones that you hear about the most. If you can find a potential undervalued property, it can work in your favor. However, you have to make sure that it will work for you.

Having undervalued property may not be in every investor's best interest. It's also good to have resources available so that you are able to increase the value on it and eventually come out with a profit.

Investing in real estate is not a new path to financial success. It is a well worn path and it is so well worn because it is such an effective way to make a great deal of money in a relatively short period of time. But you have to be a forward thinker to make any serious money in the buying and selling of real estate.

The objective is to buy low and sell high and that means that you have to make a guess (an EDUCATED guess) as to what is GOING to happen tomorrow or next week or next year or ten years from now and not base your decisions on what happened yesterday, or last week, or last year or ten years ago.

Think about the neighborhood that you grew up in. Your mom and dad bought the house when the subdivision was new. It isn't new anymore. It isn't on its way UP. It is on its way DOWN.

The residents and the buildings are all beginning to show their age. That is the nature of real estate. What goes up will eventually go down. You always want to buy when the area is on the rise and not when it is in decline. There are, of course, exceptions to this rule but there aren't many.

In short; you need to find the hot markets when buying investment property and in a nutshell the hot market is where the people are GOING. Determining where people are going is the trick. With rents going up all over, people are going everywhere so almost any rental is a good rental.

Buying in an area that is already popular can be a hot market providing you can make a good deal on the property but finding out about upcoming changes in the infrastructure can lead you to where people will be going in the future. Infrastructure changes are such things as major highway construction, marinas or entertainment facilities. Basically, you base your real estate market investments upon the cold hard facts and not what you hope will happen or what your barber tells you.

Right now isn't a great time to invest in real estate in the USA but there are hot properties overseas that you can take full advantage of while you wait for the US real estate market to recover. Costa Rica is a good example.

Costa Rica is only 3 hours from the mainland. It is a hugely popular vacation destination and beach front property has been on an upward spiral for several years but it appears that the trend is going to continue.

Real estate investing is not an exact science. You always have to weigh the risk against the potential reward and if you do decide to invest in overseas property it is wise to employ a local attorney to oversee the process.

Then there is always the 'cool' factor that shouldn't be overlooked when searching for hot investment real estate. For example: in California there is an area called 'the

Venice Beach' area. There was a film made there a few years ago that was loaded with skate boarders and surfers. Suddenly, Venice Beach became a very 'cool' place to live and real estate prices soared! So don't overlook 'cool'.

Keep both eyes on large corporation expansion plans. When corporations build, expand or even relocate the real estate market will boom simply because of demand for housing and small businesses. If a Wal-Mart is going to be built in a town, can a McDonald's be far behind? And all of those people who will be coming in to run Wal-Mart and all of the small businesses that it spawns will need housing.

Yes! Business can cause real estate prices to go up and can create hot properties for investment purposes!

Remember that old song that Willie Nelson recorded, "You have to know when to hold 'em, know when to fold 'em, know when to walk away and know when to run". Although the song was about gambling the advice is solid for investing in real estate.

Choosing what properties and locations to invest in should be made strictly upon solid facts. A building permit for a marina is solid proof that a marina is going to be built and that the adjacent property values are going to go up.

Your cousin telling you that he HEARD that a marina was going to be built is NOT a fact. Its hearsay and you shouldn't lean a lot on hearsay! Investing in real estate is an excellent way to get a very high return but you really do need to know what you are doing to keep from losing your shirt.

07

HOW TO AVOID POTENTIAL INVESTMENT TRAPS

One thing you don't want to do is to get in an investment deal that doesn't turn out right, or at least the way you thought. After all of that work, sweat and tears of finding a place, the last thing you need is a potential real estate nightmare. Here are some things you can do to help yourself steer clear of that:

- Make sure that you have the correct information regarding the property. Don't rely on the listings alone. Make phone calls and better yet, make sure to go and visit the property in question. It may or may not look like as was described in the listing.

- Walk through the property to make sure that it is what you're looking for. Don't settle for less than what you want. You will only end up disappointed.

It's ok to have a property with small repairs or upgrades to make for your first time.

- Stay away from the ones that require extensive work. That can mean you will be paying out lots of money to have stuff repaired and upgraded, or either get a loan for the repair work.

- If you have to get a mortgage loan for the property, make sure that it is one that you can afford to pay back every month. The financing should be acceptable in terms that will fit you.

- Don't sign paperwork that you don't understand so you can rush and get your first piece of real estate property. Ask questions so you will know how this will affect you financially down the road. If you don't, you can end up paying more money than you would like to.

In regard to real estate investing, go over everything about prospective property, the taxes, the loan and whatever else needs to be included. You want your first piece of real estate property to be something that you can be proud of. You also want to be able to be comfortable in paying the mortgage on it every month until it is paid off.

08

REAL ESTATE INVESTING: FULL TIME - PART TIME OR ANYTIME?

Unless you have a lot of money up front, don't think that you will be able to abruptly quit your full-time job for real estate investing. It's important that you have that financial backup because if you don't, you can get yourself into a deep, financial hole.

Plus, you don't know how long it will take you to get your first real estate property. It may take several months before you get that piece of prime real estate that you've been looking for. Start out part-time with real estate investing. That way, you won't create a burden that can drive you into insanity.

Looking for property to use as a real estate investment takes time and research. You will have to conduct due diligence to make sure that the property is what it claims to be in the real estate listing. Even though with the internet you can look at real estate properties online, you will still want to go in person to check it out for yourself. A photo can only do so much justice.

Going part-time is the wise way to go. You only have to expend so much energy per day, or however many times you look for rental properties each week. In the meantime, you will still have your full-time job and bringing in regular income.

There are times when you may hit the jackpot with a rental property, but it is only for a brief time. The tenant may move out on you or something else could happen. Then you would be back to square one, with a rental property, but no renters. That also creates loss of income for you.

If you have a mortgage with this property, you will still have to pay the monthly note, utility bills and other miscellaneous items. That's why it's so crucial to have a financial backup plan and some money to show for it. Having a negative cash flow from your rental property is not a good thing to have.

Take your time acquiring real estate investments. They are never in short supply. There is always an area where you will be able to find something to your liking. Doing this part-time allows you to test the waters to see if this is for you.

You have to be sure that this is what you want. In the beginning, real estate investing can be rather time consuming. You have to make sure that you are up for the challenge.

HIRING A HOME INSPECTOR – IS IT WORTH IT?

In order for your real estate investment to be profitable, it's a good idea to hire an experienced and qualified inspector for the property you are looking to purchase. They will be able to advise you whether or not the property is worth buying for real estate investing.

An inspector can find things that usually other people miss. They can find things that can turn into a potential larger issue if not taken care of. Some of the things that they check are:

- Electricity

- Plumbing

- Heating

- Air Conditioning

- Vents

- Water

- General upkeep of the home, including the inside and outside structure

They are trained to spot problems that you wouldn't think of. When they tell you what's wrong in the home, you can either have repairs done or change your mind about getting the property. Inspectors can help you save a lot of money when they find things that other people don't find when going through a property.

You can consult with a real estate agent about hiring an inspector. They may know several of them that can be recommended to you. Or, if you wish, do your own detective work and find one on your own. However, since agents are in this business, it may be better if you get a recommendation from them. It would also be quicker.

The inspector should thoroughly check the property inside and out. They should also think about what results you would want from the inspection. They may ask you questions to see what you're missing about the process.

Having an inspector checking your potential property is very important. They will be able to advise you of the condition of the home and whether or not it is worth purchasing, in their opinion. They are an independent party, so their recommendations are usually worth their weight in gold.

However, before you sign on the dotted line, go over everything with the inspector. They will explain in detail all of their findings from the property inspection. Then you will have to decide if this is something worth investing in.

10

MORTGAGES FOR REAL ESTATE INVESTMENTS AND SPECULATORS

In the event that you have to get a mortgage for your first real estate investment property, take your time to look at the different choices available. Of course, it helps to have great credit. The better your credit, the better chance you have of getting the loan that you want. Here are some choices when it comes to getting a mortgage loan for your property:

Fixed Mortgage

A fixed rate mortgage usually lasts for 30 years and doesn't change, hence the term "fixed rate". This is the mother of mortgage loans. For a long time, real estate investors were only able to get this kind of loan.

When they get this fixed mortgage loan, it comes with a fixed rate that remains throughout the duration of the 30 years or less if they pay it off quicker. Upon the end of the e30-year term, the loan will be considered paid in full.

In the beginning years, the monthly loan payments are applied toward the interest of the loan. As the years pass, they are eventually applied to the principal balance. This is about the easiest loan for investors to deal with because the terms are simple.

You usually won't find anything unexpected down the road as you continue to pay it off. Real estate investors would probably want to look at paying off the loan early so they won't be saddled down with a lot of debt for a long time.

The focus of real estate investing is to create wealth, not to always have financial liabilities. When investors get wealth from real estate investing, they can enjoy it as they continue to invest in more properties.

No-Money Down Loans (Zero Investment)

This is another type of mortgage loan that can be used by real estate investors. They won't have a problem trying to get information about this kind of loan, because they are always advertised somewhere. It can sometimes be touted as one of the best loans since sliced bread. However, it's important that investors know the risks about securing this kind of loan.

Real estate investors can get this kind of loan by securing a mortgage that is 100%, or they can get what is called a "piggyback" mortgage. A piggyback mortgage is when the investor secures two mortgages at the same time and put them together.

With a piggyback mortgage, the investor gets a perk by not needing a downpayment at the closing process. Also, the investor can benefit from getting the largest amount of interest available to include in their taxes as a deduction.

Being an investor, it is not always guaranteed that you will get the entire amount financed for the loan. There are many banks and other lenders that will not provide the entire 100%. If some do decide to provide the entire thing, then they will get their share by including higher interest rates. This way, they can cover themselves because you would not have provided a down payment.

As with anything else that is zero-down, your mortgage payments will be higher than usual. If you don't have a lot of money as a financial backup, this kind of loan could hurt you in the long run.

It would take you longer to have a comfortable cash flow because you would be paying a larger amount in mortgage payments. So, you may want to think about this loan option a little harder than you would others.

However, a zero-down loan could still work out for you in terms of securing an investment property. It's up to you as to whether or not you're willing and able to take the risk.

Adjustable Rate Mortgage

Adjustable rate mortgage loans, or ARMs, as they are commonly known as, are almost as popular as fixed rate mortgages. Real estate investors are known for using these as well. If you decide on this loan, you can be assured of having a variable interest rate.

A variable interest rate is the rate that lenders charge and it often fluctuates. The rates change in accordance with the increase or decrease of interest rates in the market during that time.

It would start off with a fixed rate for a few years. Then it would go into a variable period. This means that after the fixed rate period is over, your loan rate (and monthly payment) is subject to adjusting every year.

With that, the majority of ARMs have a stopping point of how much they can change. With this loan, the rate can increase or decrease to a certain amount as long as you have it.

In the beginning, this kind of loan may include a low rate of interest. For some real estate investors, this would work for them because they may not want to hold on to the property for an extended time.

Also, when the interest rates decrease, investors can grab at the chance to get in on them. On the other hand, this loan is very risky. When interest rates increase, the investor will have to go with the flow.

The bad thing about this is they will not know in advance when the rates will increase. In reality, ARMs can be an unsure thing because you don't know how much money you will continue to pay due to the constant fluctuations.

Interest-Only Loans

Another loan that is good for real estate investors in the interest-only mortgage loan. Investors can use this loan when they are having a hard time with getting positive cash flow. This usually happens when the value of the property has increased.

Some investors normally get interest-only loans if they don't want negative cash flow, if they want to use the cash for something else, or if they're thinking about getting into property flipping for a future date.

When an investor has this kind of mortgage loan, they can hold off on principal payments for a certain period of time. It is usually no more than ten years, but could be less than that. The investor is only paying the interest and nothing else during this period.

In order to get rid of the principal in the future, the loan is amortized again after the period of only paying the interest has ended. The investor ends up paying a higher mortgage loan payment. There are several ways that the investor can handle this situation: sell their property, stick with the higher payment or try to refinance.

Hard Money & Balloon Mortgages

Having a hard money loan or having balloon mortgages are not popular kinds of mortgage loans, but real estate investors have used them over and over again. This mortgage will increase using a longer time than the actual mortgage term. The investor ends up with a smaller starting payment. Hard money loans are high interest loans for short periods of time.

However, at the term's end, there will be a balance that the investor has to pay in full or refinance the loan. If the investor can't pay the lump sum in full or get refinancing, they will end up selling the property.

Even though there is an advantage for smaller mortgage payments in the beginning, at the end, the investor can come out as the loser if they can't pay off the entire balance or refinance. Plus, with refinancing, the investor will have to deal with an interest rate increase, plus refinancing costs. That's just more money coming out of their pocket than necessary.

11

CAN YOU BE A LANDLORD?

That is essentially what you will be when you have real estate properties to rent out to prospective tenants. Before you leap into the world of collecting rents and dealing with renters' issues, you have to know that going into this you will need patience and understanding.

Along with that, being a landlord also means you will:

- Work together to solve problems regarding the property

- Learn to communicate effectively with your tenants

- Make decisions that are in the best interests of the renters and your investment properties

- Want to stay in it for the long haul, especially if you're looking to create wealth

Other than rent, there will be times that the renters will contact you regarding the investment property. Sometimes it may be regarding a repair in the home. Other times it may be regarding the tenants themselves. Of course, you may get a tenant that pays their rent late or will try to skip out on paying it and disappear from the property.

However, once you are able to establish a relationship with the renters, they may find you easy to work with. In order for the cash flow to be consistent, you must be willing to some type of communication with them, instead of just looking for that rent payment on the 1st, 3rd or 5th of the month.

Be respectful to your tenants. After all, they are the ones that are helping you to create wealth (monthly rent). If they call you, return their phone calls as soon as you can. If repairs are needed in and on the property, get the appropriate people to do them.

Let your tenant know that you care about them and that you appreciate them selecting your property to live in. Remember, they can always find somewhere else to live and make another investor wealthy. Effective communication is the key.

12

SCREENING PROSPECTIVE TENANTS FOR YOUR RENTAL PROPERTY

Back in the day, you could put up a "For Rent" sign in the window or front yard of the property and get a decent tenant in no time. Or there would be advertisements in the newspaper. However, with the times changing and people not as trustworthy, real estate investors now have to use modern technology and other tools to screen for potential renters.

Along with the screening come legal issues that you as a real estate investor need to know about upfront before you start the process. That would include:

- How the screening is done

- Housing laws (both state and federal)

- Advertising without deception

It's a good idea to read up on the policies and procedures regarding this. Knowing the information beforehand can save you from potential litigation and shelling out thousands of dollars. If you are still not sure, hire an attorney that specializes in this area.

When a real estate investor or landlord wants to screen potential tenants, some of the things they should know about include:

- Employment

- Current income

- Credit history

- Previous rental history (including any evictions)

The prospective tenant needs to fill out an application. The application should be completed in full. Anything that does not apply to them should be marked with a dash or N/A (not applicable). Go over the application to make sure it is correctly filled out. Ask the applicant to provide you with character references that can be checked.

Ask for a photo ID to make sure that the person is who they say they are. The ID, such as a driver's license, should be valid. Copy the driver's license number on the application.

Let the prospective tenant know that you will have a background check as well as a credit check done. This can help you to weed out any potential problem renters. They will have to provide their consent for the credit check.

Set up a time to meet with your prospective tenants in person. In the world of modern technology, face-to-face meetings can get pushed to the back burner. However, meeting them in person can show you their personality and if they are someone you would want to rent your property to.

On the application, have a code of conduct that they are to adhere by should you allow them to rent from you. The code of conduct will also include what is expected of you and what is expected of the tenant. Make sure it is explained in a manner where they can understand it. If you're not sure about the wording, seek counsel from a real estate attorney that specializes in this.

One of the most important things that you must do is to follow the policies and procedures of the Fair Housing

Act, or FHA. This helps to keep you in line as well as protect prospective tenants from being discriminated due to race, religion, gender, disability, sexual orientation, etc.

Read over the policies carefully. You may have to read them several times to make sure you understand and avoid unnecessary litigation. You must work to avoid the appearance of being biased in any way, shape, form or fashion.

13

CALCULATING MONTHLY RENT

In order to determine how much rent to charge, there are a number of things that factor into this. First you have to look at the supply and demand within the real estate market. There may be other real estate properties similar to yours, but do you know how many there are?

You may have a tough time if you find out that there are plenty of vacancies for the taking. For you, that also means that you will be facing steep competition from others who are trying to do the same thing. You may have to consult with experienced real estate professionals to assist you with this.

Do you have property in an area where it is booming or do you have more people moving out? You will be able to provide good rental prices if the area is stable and on the upswing.

Depending on what will benefit you, you may choose lower rental prices over higher ones, and vice versa. One thing that you will need to do is to check out other properties and find out what they are renting for. Get a real estate agent to assist you. They have the tools where they can get information on the prices of home in nearby neighborhoods.

If you see some "For Rent" signs, then you may want to call the number to inquire about how much the property is being rented for. Search online for tools that can help you get comparable rental prices for similar properties in the area. Don't forget about the MLS system.

Once you have come up with a price for the rent and put it in place, you will have to work on maintaining a profit. Initially, you may not see much, but as different things happen, such as inflation and the like, you will have more expenses and your taxes will increase.

However, you can counter that by raising the rent. After the end of the current term is when the rent increase would take place and start with the new term. You want to keep the tenants that you have so that the cash flow will continue to come in. In order to do that, you must keep the lines of communication open with them. Once you cut it off, they will be more tempted to leave.

14

HAVING REPAIRS DONE ON BUDGET

There is no doubt that with a home, something will eventually need to be repaired. Anything that is physical is subject to break or get out of shape at any given time. People live in homes and things will break.

As a real estate investor, you are obligated to make sure that your tenants are not living in danger. It is important when something is reported as needing to be repaired, that you will step up to the task.

Or at least use funds to get a professional to do the repairs, which is probably a better idea anyway. Some investors wouldn't dare touch a nail, let alone a hammer, which in reality, can keep them from getting burned out.

Even before you purchase the real estate property, you need to include repairs. Something is always going to need to be repaired or replaced, no matter what. That's just the nature of the real estate investing business.

Repairs may be one of the last things that investors think about, if at all. What's more important to them is making sure they receive their rent payments on time, paying taxes and other related issues regarding money. Of course, that's important too, but it's usually the little things that they don't think about until something happens.

As a potential real estate investor, it's important that you look at the property carefully before you rent it out to a tenant. Having an inspector can serve as a backup. They can help you find more things that need to be addressed.

Some of those are minor cosmetic issues, others can be a little more serious. Either way, it's important that you have funds set aside for repairs and replacements.

Be careful when it comes to this. You don't want to purchase a property that requires a massive reworking and repair. That will not only cost you time, but it will also cost you money. If you don't have the funds on reserve up front, then you will find yourself strapped for cash.

That's one reason why it is stressed that you as an investor have a reserve of funds set aside in advance. Set a budget for repair and replacement work. Otherwise, you should bypass that property and find one where you may have to do minor work on it. Also, when a repair has to be done, get it taken care of as quickly as possible so conditions won't worsen.

15

BUYING A PROPERTY THAT WILL GENERATE POSITIVE CASH FLOW

When looking at real estate properties as financial investments, you will have to decide whether an appreciated value or positive cash flow is your main goal for getting properties. There are some things you need to consider before you make that decision.

Since you would more than likely be looking at single family homes and multifamily homes, there is a difference between the two.

With the former, the value of the property usually increases in value quicker. However, since more expenses are attached, you may not be looking at the kind of positive cash flow that you want.

On the other hand, multifamily units (i.e., duplexes) can generate more positive cash flow. However, they may not appreciate quickly like single-family homes do. Also, not as many expenses are attached to the latter.

Since most real estate investors look to create wealth, they will choose having a positive cash flow. In this case, you will need a reliable real estate agent that is willing to help you find real estate properties that will produce the positive cash flow you want.

Look at the balance sheets and see what you will look forward to as far as repairs, maintenance, fees and other miscellaneous expenses.

In order to maintain a steady stream of positive cash flow, you need to have the right tenants, so take your time. There are some people who will spend lots of money on real estate courses that don't teach much of anything.

They end up being back at square one. Find a good real estate agent that is willing to genuinely help you. Sometimes, you may be fortunate enough to find one that is also an investor on the side.

Calculating Your Cash Flow

As a real estate investor, you need to be able to calculate all of the cash flow that comes from your properties. You want to make sure that you are making a profit. You will also be able to make decisions on real estate investments that you may purchase in the future.

In order to calculate your cash flow, you will need to add up how much rent you will get from your tenants. If you have more than one unit, take into consideration any vacancies you may have. Depending on how your property looks, include a small percentage of the vacancy rate into the equation.

With the total rental amount, get a figure for your losses. You will have to include property expenses, mortgage loan interest and property depreciation.

Deduct the expenses from your total rental income in order to get your losses or savings for taxes. With that, you will either add or deduct that from your expected amount from your tenants. Take your operating expenses and monthly mortgage payment(s) and deduct them for a second time. The result will be your cash flow.

When you come up with a cash flow amount, you will be able to figure out how much you will charge for rent if you decide to purchase future real estate properties. It's important that whatever money you make, that you don't squander it. Put it away because eventually you will need it for other things relating to your investment properties.

Changing Negative Cash Flow to Positive Cash Flow

When you have negative cash flow, you are not making a profit. You are paying out more in expenses than you are taking in as profit. That's not how you want to operate when you're investing in real estate properties.

Here are some ways that you can chance the negative cash flow to a positive one:

- Implement a rent increase. Only increase it to the amount of the current market. Don't overdo it, other wise you may not have any tenants.

- Make the tenants pay the utilities. This would relieve a burden from you. Besides, since they are living in your property, they will be using utilities every day.

- Go over your property taxes to see if you can find anything that may have been missed before. Who knows—you may find out that you were charged more in taxes than you should have been charged.

- Contact your insurance company and see about paying more for your deductible. Then make inquiries about getting a better deal for coverage on the property.

16

OTHER TIPS ABOUT REAL ESTATE INVESTING

It can't be stressed enough that when you're starting out, don't rush to get the first piece of property that you see. It's important that you conduct your due diligence with everything regarding real estate investing.

Even though it is a lucrative and profitable business, you can also lose money if you don't work it properly. Don't listen to all of those stories that you hear about people making lots of money "overnight" with real estate investing. It takes more than a day to start seeing a profit. It can take more than a week to actually get a property that you want and can afford to get.

If you take your time and look around, you may be surprised as to how much is available to you in terms of real estate properties. There seems to never be a shortage of places where you can find a place to use for a profitable investment.Once you get into real estate investing, it's important to stay in it for the long haul. That's the way you will create wealth. Regardless of whether the market is up or down, you must be willing to weather any storms that come about. There will be times when there are down markets, but you can't give up and throw in the towel.

It seems like those that are getting their feet wet want to get in when the iron is hot, but when it gets cold, they want to bail out. Gaining lucrative wealth from real estate investing comes with staying the course. Even in downtimes, you can still profit. There will always be people that are looking for a place to live.

You will be able to increase rent as time goes on. This will help you produce a surplus while you are still paying the same amount on your mortgage loan. This of course, can happen if you have a structured loan payment that doesn't fluctuate during any given period.

Getting into real estate investing can be a good experience for you. You would be learning one of the best ways to build up wealth.

Since you are not Superman, don't expect to do all of the repairs yourself. There may be some minor cosmetic issues you can take care of. Other than that, leave it up to the professionals. You don't want to get burned out before you get your feet wet.

It takes a lot to maintain and manage real estate properties. When you get to the point where you have a nice cash flow every month, you can hire a property management company to do the work for you. This will free you from the tasks that you would get used to doing yourself. That would include getting rental payments and dealing with various tenant issues.

When you do decide to purchase property for investing purposes, seek counsel from those who have come before you. It's important that you have adequate information before you jump into something like this. Real estate investing involves time and money. You need both in order to make this business work for you and you not working for it.

Find experienced investors that are willing to spend some time with you showing you some of the ins and outs of real estate investing. They can share some of their experiences with you and advise you on what to look out for. In addition to repairs, you will need to keep enough funds on hand in order to honor your mortgage loan obligations on time.

Having adequate knowledge prior to making that leap into a venture like this can help you avoid the pitfalls that can befall some new real estate investors. Getting into real estate investing can be exciting and lucrative, but you have to be willing to deal with the negatives as well as the positives.

Have realistic goals and remember that real estate investing is a process. Those who claimed to have gotten their wealth quickly through real estate investing probably don't have it now.

Most of all try to keep an open mind and don't get yourself worked up when things go wrong, as they will when you have tenants. If you do your homework, you can avoid some of the issues that can happen to investors.

Getting the right tenant for your properties can sometimes be a hassle. However, it's better to take your time and get the right people so you can avoid a major headache later. You can get a sense of the kinds of people that would make good tenants.

They will have stability with their place of employment and have not hopped around like a rabbit, living in different places. Getting someone that has a good stability record is one of the main keys that can help you to get them as a tenant.

Another thing you need to think about is not trying to hoard a bunch of properties at once. Start out with one and then work your way up. Working at a slower pace will help you to properly maintain and manage what you have.

You will be successful once you employ strategies that take you from one step to the next. It's better to have properties that will provide you with a steady income than waiting on the next blockbuster that may take a while, meaning years to come. That's a negative cash flow scenario waiting to happen.

After you feel comfortable with the first one, then you may want to look for the next one, and so on. This will help you to appreciate your investments better as opposed to being in a hurry to make money and acquire wealth.

Be better than your competition. Don't just put up a sign and hope that people will come. You have to market and advertise. You may need to place ads in the paper and get with seasoned real estate professionals to help you.

Not everyone you ask will be willing to step up to the plate, but you will find a few that won't mind spending time to help you along the way. Of course, you still have to conduct your due diligence.

Eventually, you will have so many investment properties, you won't have a choice but to hire a property management company to take over. Of course, you will have to set aside funds to pay them for their services. That's all the more reason for you to take it easy when it comes to building wealth with real estate investments.

Before you know it, you'll be on your way to building wealth with real estate investment properties all over.

GOOD LUCK AND GOD BLESS YOU! IF YOU FOUND ANY VALUE IN THIS BOOK PLEASE DO ME THE HONOR OF LEAVING A BOOK REVIEW. THANK YOU AND HAVE A GREAT DAY!

www.ingramcontent.com/pod-product-compliance
Lightning Source LLC
Chambersburg PA
CBHW071501210326
41597CB00018B/2643